Copyright © 2018 Tekkan
Artwork Copyright © 2018

All rights reserved.
First Printing, 2018
ISBN 978-1-7324107-0-1

To contact Tekkan please email:
buddhaboy1289@gmail.com

How to Read My Poems

I have married the sonnet to the tanka. I tell a story in the sonnet — using three quatrains, separated by line spaces, and a final couplet. The story builds to a conclusion in the couplet. The tanka is a commentary, or a counterpoint, to the sonnet — the combined poems have two endings.

I don't rhyme my sonnets, because I want freer expression. I want to be direct in my meaning — I want people to clearly understand my meaning. The metaphors are inspired by Shakespeare, and the (aimed-for) precision is in imitation of Japanese style. Using the sonnet with the tanka, I am mixing the sensibility of the Occident and the Orient — which I have done by living in England, Japan, and America.

I don't punctuate much in my poetry. I want the words themselves to do the work. There is logic between words, and the forms provide structure. By not using punctuation I hope to direct readers to carefully attend to each word — to appreciate the graininess of words.

Reading my poems silently, say, on a bus, a train, or an airplane, and reading them aloud, may be different experiences. The way I've written there's not always a pause intended at the end of the line. Hint: *My poems are to be recited not as lines, but as phrases, and a phrase often overflows the break at the end of a line. I pause and take a breath where it seems natural for me to pause. Another person may pause differently than I do.*

Each single poem is a piece of a mosaic, and it is my hope that the collection of poems form an accurate portrait of consciousness.

My daughter, Jocelyn MacDonald, is a wonderful artist. Her art work graces this book.

I am Barry MacDonald. I received the *dharma* name, *Tekkan*, which means, Iron Man, a settled practitioner of great determination.

— *Tekkan*

Everyday Mind I

To woo
women

is to
play

and sus-
pend

the
moment;

one

doesn't

hold

control.

June is a memory in November
As I remember the roses and the
Lilacs blooming and the persistence of
The rain the fresh air and the insistence

Of the sun coaxing the season of growth
Along and all the leaves are pristine the
Birds are melodious with the dawn and
The roots of the grass are absorbing the

Rain but now a bitter wind surges through
The trees that stand starkly bare a frosting
Has hardened the ground and the night has grown
Wings and is overshadowing daylight

But none of it matters to me because
Your ebullience overcomes the darkness.

The overcast sky
in November is glowing
because the sun is
always dispensing light and
every day you're radiant.

Stillwater

Iced-over river and overcast sky
Slopes of bare trees and snow the clean cold air
The quiet settled among the bluffs
Prepare this place for reverberations

When the native peoples walked for water
The valley they called "Stillwater" was here
Resonating with creeks and waterfalls
As water spread between limestone bluffs

Sioux and Ojibwa fought in a hollow
Lumberjacks floated rafts of logs downstream
A frontier prison held the Younger Gang
And steamboats plied the townsfolk with supplies —

Pioneer Park has a southward view
For sunrises and sun speckled water.

Sun river
eagle soaring
seeing.

Volition

Mrs. Peterson encouraged me in
High school to read and in the library
I found *Siddhartha* a novel about
An Indian prince contemporary

With the Buddha who began questing for
Awakening by leaving home entering
The woods and meditating and the tale
Inexplicably resonated with

Me and a seed was planted that sprouted
Twenty years later while I taught English
In Japan and met Jim Morton who led
Me to *Hosshinji* a monastery

Where I began seeking enlightenment
Wholeheartedly some thirty years ago.

A leaf opens
to the sun
and I opened
to words
of inspiration.

I like the simplicity of coming
To my *zafu* and *zabuton* on the
Floor sitting with my legs crossed with a straight
Back with my shoulders relaxed and I like

Following my breath and balancing my
Attention allowing thoughts to arise
And letting them go without becoming
Emotional if possible because

I'm sitting as impassively as I
Can but if I become agitated
I practice letting go with the practice
Of motionless posture as if I were

A mountain weathering a thunderstorm
And practice breathing and practice breathing.

Sitting
agitated until
agitation goes
is simple but
not easy.

My mind is a bowl pondering why my
Friend would say he has no one he relies
On because he's never said such hurtful
Words before and my mind is a bowl of

Frustration as I'm plotting to persuade
A woman to submit to my way of
Managing our meager finances as
I consider her quirky reactions

And my mind is a bowl seeing the sun
In a brilliant sky amidst moving clouds
And there suspended is a crescent moon
And for moment I'm just watching as

My mind is a bowl and an opening
Offering good intentions this morning.

Crescent moon
is a hole
in the day
of a blue sky.

As if you and I were assembling
A puzzle together finding pieces
Of our lives scattered on a table and
While drinking coffee we were perusing

Segments of experience and with joy
We discovered commonality and
Compatibility quite surpassing
Ordinary friendliness and so I

Relied on our partnership over time
As we kept connecting the puzzle but
One day you became unapproachable
For no discernable reason I could

Fathom as our friendship dissolved on a
Saturday and you became the puzzle.

Searching for
wholeness
companionship
I want direction
home.

A yellow light spreads on the horizon
As a transparent layering of clouds
Disintegrates in the blue of the sky
Producing tiny crystals of snow as

The sun is rising and snow is shining
The whole sky is changing and who would care
To notice this daily transformation as
Usually I'm busy in traffic or

Immersed in the political news but
See how the sun is a brilliant yellow
The sky has opened and an airliner has
Streaked across leaving contrails drifting and

Seeing the magic in a moment I've
Forgotten ordinary compulsions.

Survival requires
vigorous mastery of
focused energy
yet I want to cultivate
a disengaging talent.

The morning sun shone on the snow on the
Ground and for a moment hundreds of the
Crystals sparkled and the snow became a
Blanket of jewels — in the afternoon as

I drove through town I saw an apple tree
At a modest home decorated with
Dozens of Christmas bulbs in bare branches
Projecting a holiday vibe for me

And even though I was enduring a
Season of scant sun and frigidity
When any exposed skin burned with the cold
As I waited for the heater in my

Car to heat I generated a glow
Of quiet satisfaction and patience.

It takes discipline
to move about in winter
but even amidst the
most austere landscape there are
visions of joyous beauty.

My mind is a bowl of below zero
Cold as I'm following boot prints in the
Shining snow under a blue sky as I'm
Enveloped in a coat with only my

Face burning a little — my mind is a
Bowl and my spine is a staff and my crossed
Legs are foundational for arising
Energy as time and thought are slowed in

Zen — my mind is a bowl and an apple
Tree with half a dozen chickadees just
For a moment as they flutter and go
As I watch from my window and I can

Think of nothing worthier then the birds
As an offering for you this morning.

With nothing between
me and the world I can see
chickadees in the
apple tree and I needn't
think about significance.

The swallow bursts before me snatching my
Sight swooping rising diving and turning
Turning as if it were a whirling blade
Turning and then vanishing into sky —

But the bumblebee lumbers in the grass
Plodding and bumbling and purposeful
Desirous of nectar to return home
Serving the manufacture of the hive —

I can't resist the urge to grab the toad
Squeezing and turning it as I wonder
Is it toads or frogs that give out warts and
I suppose it's either but I don't care —

I've spent an hour playing in summer
And so escaped a dreary winter day.

These blasted days
have frozen my toes
my constantly frozen
toes until this morning's
thaw.

Eric

I remember my first friend beyond my
Family the first intimacy when
We discovered there were secrets to share
And with innocence I gave my trust and

I encountered how much fun it was to
Delve and roam the neighborhood and then my
Family moved to Minnesota and
I left my friend in Kansas — and there was

A procession of friendships and there were
Disappointments and betrayals and I
Had to grow a layer of armor and
I began to measure how much trust was

Sensible and I've tasted bitterness —
But I want to be gentle and sincere.

Wholehearted
innocence was
lost — but I have
circumspection
and kindness.

It's a modest dining room a smallish
Round table and in the morning I make
Coffee and have a bowl of cereal —
Maybe a conversation an email

Or an expression on someone's face from
The day before has left an impression
With me and so I consider what they
Are thinking and how they are coping and

What I should do — I didn't understand
How to direct my energy when young
How to discover what needs attention —
I come to my breakfast table as to

A reliable sanctuary and
Continuously find intuition.

Solitude is good
regularity helpful
quiet conducive
for the cultivation of
insightful understanding.

The Accident

As winter is dragging on and darkness
Is dominating morning and evening
I became frustrated being stuck in
The little rooms within my little house

So I was blasé this morning in the
Bathroom when I opened the cabinet
And the trimmer fell out into the sink
And I didn't care and I didn't think

Until I trimmed off half my beard and I
Realized the fall had changed the settings
And then what could I do but shave the rest
Even though I was watching the daily

Progression of my winter beard and now
I have to begin all over again.

Or maybe not but
I will certainly
go to a barber
to get a haircut
and restore balance.

To live in proximity with you for
Thirty years has determined so much of
What's emerged as I'm driving you to work
Because your car's being repaired with my

Habitual quiet with you chatting
About who's gossiping about whom and
Who's attending to their cell phones and not
Working about the squirrel you've named "Chub

Chub" that some of you are feeding by the
Dumpster about what you set your heart on
About how you formulate words about
My mind wandering and you asking a

Question and it's hard to imagine
The ride going another direction.

So we discuss what's
going to happen later in
the day when you need
picking up and when we need
to do the weekly shopping.

Balancing so I hear you and not the
Television balancing so I hear
The meaning of your words before forming
A response balancing how I wanted

To use this time with your apparent need
To communicate now balancing so
I see my thinking and emotion so
My behavior is appropriate so

I'll have no cause for regret and so I
May see how I might do something worthy
To alleviate conflicting schedules
Or perhaps to just listen to you share

Your experience of this day because
It's so important to live together.

An everyday poise
opening awareness
seeing within me
and seeing circumstances
is a transforming practice.

So it swells into a drop of water
Precariously under the faucet
Separating and falling and bursting
With a plunk in the hollow of the sink

And I can't think of anything to do
To prevent the next drop from forming and
Plunking in the sink except to call a
Plumber as the monotonous plopping

Punctuates the spacious kitchen with a
Plink pointing to a problem needing a
Solution I don't have as I'm not so
Mechanically inclined but suddenly

I remember to get the pliers and
Unscrew the ending and clean the filter.

I've reestablished
quiet and serenity
in the household but
I don't smile triumphantly
As who knows what's coming next?

I couldn't get you to be quiet and
Couldn't persuade you not to lash out at
Him couldn't even intervene to keep
The two of you from arguing as I

Was witnessing the obvious damage
Occurring as both of you were building
Resentments deepening a pattern that
Has disrupted your lives so I will look

For an opening when I can say please
Try to forget about who's right and wrong
Try to regain some composure because
It's much more important at the moment —

But I know from experience there's not
Much I can do to keep you from fighting.

When I'm the target
of someone's anger I want
to fight back even
though I see generations
perpetuating anger.

Suppose there's no death suppose consciousness
Continuously cycles in lifetimes
Meandering in a loopy sort of
Way while the attributes you think

Are so quintessentially you such as
The shapeliness of your body such as the
Suppleness of your mind such as your face
In the mirror are recycled in the

Round do you think your personality
Would persist or is it possible that
Your consciousness and your eyesight
Would be adapting to a different world

With a novel set of inclinations
Or would you face the same old conundrums?

Speculation is
amusing but has limits —
I like ponderous
suppositions but now I
have my chores to finish.

I had a friend who was a poet who
Was terrified by the oblivion
Of space and by Nazi atrociousness
And his fear assumed an angry guise when

Encountering those of lighter views and
He wasn't blaming anyone but he
Believed God was absent and life was cruel
And so he embodied bitterness I

Believe he embraced and he despaired for
Himself for his friends as his mind was a
Whirlpool sinking to a void but as for
Me I suppose we're spirits persisting

In eternity and we have questions
To address and choices to determine.

I see
I question
the birthing of
my eyesight
my questioning.

Temple Eihei-ji

What could a Japanese temple on a
Mountain built in the thirteenth century
Have to do with me — and in ignorance
I lived at the mountain's base and I would

Climb for exercise following a worn
Trail but only on the last day did I
Find the temple entrance — the monk Dogen
Returned from China with empty hands and

The *dharma* and he chose the mountaintop
As a sanctuary and he filled a
Room with candlelight and ever since then
Candles and the *dharma* have been burning —

In America we have the light too
Because Dogen transmitted the knowledge.

So nonsensical
so initially absurd —
what's there to gain by
sitting silently for hours —
there's really nothing to gain.

"Life of Pi"

As yellow staring eyes transfix the goat
It becomes arrow straight and its shoulders
And hips move not very noticeably
In the line of advance the tiger comes

Directly forward moving purposefully
Carefully slowly placing its paws
In a rhythm of attack low to the
Floor and paralyzing the goat the tiger

Comes with its yellow staring eyes and its
Open mouth and its fangs and its stripes it's
Mesmerizing and alarming in waves
The tethered bleating goat knowing there's no

Escaping — the tiger snaps the goat's neck
And drags it along the length of the cage.

In the movie a
father who manages a
zoo showed his son a
tiger is not a thing that
thinks like us — it's not a friend.

Temple Wat Pha Luang

In Thailand poachers killed the adults and
The villagers didn't know what to do
With the tiger cubs so they took them to
A Buddhist temple for the monks to take

Care of and because they're given only
Cooked meat they don't acquire a taste for blood
And so the temple's become a home to
A procession of tigers and monks who

Mingle as if the imperatives of
Violence would disintegrate before
Loving kindness as if benevolence
And compassion were persuasive as if

Buddhism had impetus to turn the
Primordial to a gentle tiger.

So evidently
evolutionary fact
is not conclusive
and a tigerish impulse
can be overcome with love.

Nothing is like an onrushing cold for
Grabbing attention as I felt it in
My throat in my voice when I tried to speak
Especially in my nose which began

To run and mostly in my noggin which
Became seasick and then there were the times
When I rose from bed once the congestion
Had taken hold and my back and shoulders

Felt sore my head throbbed as I went to the
Rest room but there is a lighter side to
Getting sick as it took me out of my
Daily routine separating me from

The hamster wheel of doing the same things
Day after day exertion without thought.

Recovery's not
quite like returning from a
vacation but it
is a rediscovery
of marvelous energy.

I can find a sense of solemnity
Without being a sour puss if I
Recognize the consequences of my
Thoughts and words with people as I often

Underestimate how easily an
Unappealing attitude becomes known
By the slightest gestures of my body
As I am a transmitter of moods and

A recipient of the subtlest
Messages and if I'm kind harmony
Manifests and if grumpy obstacles
Appear as there's a sacred quality

To human interaction as we do
Impact each other for better or worse.

Without intention
my face reveals secrets
without reflection
I don't know what I'm doing —
communication happens.

What is there in a name as I think of
You and your parents at your christening
As they gave you a lovely name in a
Traditional ceremony as a

Bestowal of their best intentions for
You as if they could be present smoothing
Your passage in a life that could involve
Precarious episodes as if they

Could enfold you within the love of Christ
By simply selecting "Kristine" as if
The repetition of your name might serve
As an incantation that would impart

Magical protection throughout your life
Because they won't be with you forever.

A name is a gift
and a reflection of your
parents' desires —
they wished you inspiration
encompassing a lifetime.

There's a rhythm to a running printing
Press and once the settings are right and the
Rollers are inked the paper's loaded and
The copy's been transformed into a plate

And fitted to the roller I can turn
The switch to see the paper raised and fed
And dropped at the other end and then the
Fun begins as adjustments are made and

The image must be good and it takes a
Practiced eye and a head full of knowledge
To a keep a press producing wonderful
Product as chemicals are managed and

Machinery is maintained and the ink
And the water must flow separately.

It looks so easy
as a skilled pressman does it
as nothing goes wrong
but watch as the novice tries —
he gets smeared in printer's ink.

Who cares about compassion anyway?
In our culture it's more important to
Be right to be a leader to get things
Done and the word sounds wimpy so perhaps

It's a concern of women or clergy
But I've discovered as I care about
Myself as I have a family and
Value harmony and happiness for

My children one doesn't incorporate
Difficulties or turn from selfishness
Without understanding the suffering
Of other people and desiring

It's relief and sometimes while I'm feeling
Angry it's helpful to behave kindly.

As a child will rage
an adult could also rage
but it's much better
to turn the energy of
anger to useful purpose.

There's a division between having the
Diabetes and cancer and watching
While healthy as the misfortunes arise
Becoming too much for one to bear and

Witnessing and participating in
Suffering breaks down the dividing lines
Between us as imagination leads
To empathy leads to compassion and

Starting with a loved one understanding
Expands encompassing many and when
I discover the subtle gradations
Of dissatisfaction I realize

Everyone suffers together more or
Less and together we experience.

I was afflicted
with aggressive uniqueness
but bearing witness
helped me to understand
suffering is communal.

It's hard to get the words outside
My mouth because the aggravation builds
To belligerency and while I know
Enough not to trust my inclinations

To see the high and the low responses
Possible it's difficult to take the
Blame in a partnership that's not working
And parsing a litany of events

With an eye for justification in
Defense is not what I want to do and
From experience I know defending
Or attacking is useless and so I

Need to walk away and take the time to
Decompress to locate a friend and talk.

The rollercoaster
of entangled emotions
I've discovered takes
its time to run its course and
later normalcy returns.

Supposedly a dog's nose is hundreds
Of times better than ours and when looking
About I see the people who've mastered
Their dogs walking together side by side

While other pairs aren't so harmonious
And I wonder how the walk would go with
The dog in charge because he's not wedded
To straight lines going from here to there he's

Nosing the delectable enticements
Of the earth and we're oblivious and
We require such pitiful restraint of
Our creatures — how well would you do if we

Put a leash on you and dangled tempting
Aromas out of reach and marched on home?

Are we really the
bestest of friends or are we
ignominious
and parsimonious as our
doggies obey commandments?

A milky sky with the trees coated with
Just fallen snow is a perishable
Wonderland of an hour's duration as
The forecast temperature will reach the

Forties by afternoon as a clipper
Has passed and rain is coming but for now
I'm savoring a moment's interlude
Where the tiny apple tree the pines and

The towering cottonwood are covered
In powered sugar and the sparrow can't
Determine where to land and a squirrel's
Hop-running on the snow and there's not a

Shadow to be seen while everything is
Concealed in a blanket of glowing snow.

As I'm watching the
snow frosting is vanishing
from the limbs and twigs
of the trees and the landscape
is increasingly soggy.

Enso

A child could do it with as much pleasure
As a master with a simple motion
Of the arm holding a brush full of ink
And creating a circle on paper

And the master would know how much ink to
Use would be familiar with the motion
And would have ways of considering the
Child doesn't but in either case making

An enso is an act of creation
As the image represents the motion
Of planets the repetition of the
Seasons the circularity of life

And a child should have the experience
Of exploring with resonate symbols.

That the sun and moon
reappear everyday that
summer becomes fall
that thoughts are repetitive
points to circularity.

Once I was the planet circling you
But now I'm the sun propelling you as
I have acquired the weight and the pull
As I have watched my emotions and have

Learned to let them go as I have practiced
Loving kindness by disbelieving the
Critical mind by not opposing sharp
Thoughts but by observing and by letting them

Go as I have come not to disparage
Myself love arises naturally
And love overcomes separateness and
Love emanates outwards naturally

As light does and without intention I
Have acquired the gravity and poise.

It's not a question
of power or intention
it's the way things are
as love and light emanate
outward and acquire weight.

Think of what I could do with my fingers
As I have known a big guy with large hands
Who was capable of such delicate
Work with wood and I remember my dad

Playing the piano for hours as a
Way of engaging equanimity
And think of the type of spirit I am
To be given the tips of my fingers

For touching and the grip of my hands for
Lifting and the palms for holding that serve
As an extension of my mind that I
May explore the world and fashion a way

Of living harmonious with my thoughts
That I may handle my pressing desires.

Because my fingers
and my mind are passages
to a world filled with
possibilities that I
touch with precision and care.

Even clouds are racing as they've broken
In chunks and are chasing each other and
Even without their leaves the trees in the
Onslaught are roaring and even trunks of

The thin trees are swaying as if they were
Branches and everywhere I turn every
Tree is tossing every bush is moving
A newspaper is flying and the clouds

Are passing and their shadows are moving
But clarity brightens again with the
Sun and I have to turn my back on the
Chilly chafing blowing and I have to

Work hard to keep my balance and every
Second seems approaching a crescendo.

The snow is gone and
the landscape is barren of
growth and it appears
the wind is combing the earth
and winter is vanishing.

If I were discovering my body
As I was growing I'd jump onto the
Top of the refrigerator too and
Just for fun I might push the boxes of

Cereal off to watch them fall and hear
Them plop on the floor and thus to measure
Distance and then I'd gallop joyously
Around the rooms just because I could and

I'd strut out on the narrow ledge and knock
The knick-knacks down one-by-one just to see
Them go and I'd be curious about
The human and the funny noises and

The motions she's making with her arms and
I'd flop on my back and ask to be rubbed.

It's necessary
to be emphatic to be
noisy and grandma
isn't enough to impose
her will on the new kitten.

There are the buds appearing again on
The tips of the trees after a season
Of bareness and the growing insistence
Of the sun that is glaring is like a

Bolt from the sky that's impossible to
Ignore and I'm struck by the potency and
Persistence of the sun turning again
The wheel of the seasons to the time of

Growth and splendor and I am grateful for
The simplicity of its power that
It pours its light on the earth and the grass
Grows the trees bud and the air warms as

It does every spring and I welcome the
Return of the prominence of the light.

There was a moment
of splendor in the winter
when the shine of the
sun shone on the crystals of
the snow and pointed the light.

Crazy —

Where would I be without my sight and my
Hearing and how would I move without my
Arms and legs and what would I be thinking
Without my mind and would I be happy?

If I weren't here to experience my
Being where would I be and also if
This universe weren't here what would be and
What would nothing look like if no one were

Here to see? Does my heart beat itself or
Do I beat it and also does the sun
Burn itself and if not who does? Today
I'm happy to be alive and perhaps

I've been alive a millions times before
But I'm just not able to remember.

If I weren't here would
the earth be here without me
or does my presence
include the earth and the sun
as we create each other?

As ordinary as a squirrel as
Common as a sparrow as everyday
As a gust of wind moving the needles
Of a pine tree the world it seems wiggles

And the quiescence of the apple tree
The rose and the lilac bushes is an
Illusion as they're responding to a
More assertive sun and are preparing

Blossoms — this is where I want to be in
The morning drinking in the barest sights
And sounds because I've come to take pleasure
By noticing how a steady wind stirs

The branches of the maple the walnut
And the cottonwood and I don't need more.

My eyes touch the sun
and the sun embraces me
my ears hold the wind
and the wind caresses me
and we exist together.

Sometimes in idleness I find myself
Entering the labyrinth of my mind
Ruminating on the friendships that went
Wrong and retracing the particulars

Retelling myself the same purposeless
Stories and feeling again emotions
With no resolution and as I have
Done my praying and the amending of

Myself necessary I believe that
The arrival of forgiveness and of
Letting go isn't entirely up
To me and that ruminating with some

Sympathy and humor can be helpful —
After all these years I can be childish.

My ego cherishes
its frustrations and enjoys
replaying stories
for no useful purpose just
to create some excitement.

I wasn't there as I usually
Was when it happened I didn't hear the
Terrific bang but I saw the heavy
Cutting machine knocked into the printing

Press and the double doors bashed apart and
The tool chest askew and the bits of glass
And sheet rock everywhere and I saw the
Van where it shouldn't be in the printing

Room as Dad had lost control of the brake
And couldn't stop in the garage but smashed
The doors in for the second time within
A year but I did see him crestfallen

And tearful as he did acknowledge the
Time had come when he could no longer drive.

We were worried and
sad because he admitted
he was forgetting
his way on the city streets
he's been driving forty years.

The whole expanse of the blue sky mixes
With the trees in the park where the people
Come for these few days of the season as
This is the time of the cherry blossoms —

It's the singularity of the pink
Flowering that touches the heart with a
Color that points the year because now is
When we celebrate the lifting of the

Winter cold and the returning of warm
Breezes and the stirring of growth with a
Strengthening sun and it's natural to
Rejoice and cherish the moment of the

Cherry blooms because it may rain and the
Blossoms may separate and so vanish.

It's quite natural
when the sun strengthens again
for people to rejoice and
create a ceremony.

The blooming crabapple tree is peaking
And its blossoms are streaming in the wind
While other flowering trees and hedges
Are opening and creating such a

Captivating sight as I'm driving in
Town and I'm wondering why this slice of
Nature affects me so as mosquitoes
And wood ticks are as natural as the

Cherry blooms as common as a bout of
Frenzied thinking my mind endures and so
Maybe it's better not to question but
To appreciate the periodic

Appearance of beauty on the earth as
It blooms and then vanishes in the wind.

I can do without
the mosquitoes and wood ticks
but it is my choice
to overlook the pests and
be enamored with beauty.

That before my eyes the squirrel would run
The length of the top of the long white fence
Without stopping — and the robin would stop
In the apple tree for a brief rest and

Then fly — that the leaves are half-way growing
And the grass is rising up and the sky
Is sunny but was rainy yesterday —
And my eyes are seeing and my mind is

Absorbing the scene without distraction —
As I'm indulging the freedom to see
The thinnest of clouds disintegrating —
And I remember other seasons of

My living when I was lost in yearnings
And dissatisfactions and now I'm not.

I am the center
of my being and I may
direct attention
in whatever direction
suits me within the moment.

I gaze at the perpetrator in the
Mirror every morning and start with the
Left side of my chin with downward strokes and
Then I go under my nose and it does

Become apparent when it's time to change
The razor because a dull blade will drag
Above my lip where I am sensitive —
I could be thinking about politics

Or the Academy Awards — while on
My right side next to my ear I begin
Stroking down against the grain to my neck
Until I reach my chin and when finished

I like to put the razor down and with
My fingers I like to feel smoothiness.

I've just discovered
an oddity that's
taken forever
to notice — my right
side is hairier.

Sadly a sense of dignity comes and
Eliminates possibilities so
Adults really can't descend again to
The excitements and pleasures of childhood

Because what would it look like to see the
Usual person of middle-age girth
On the monkey bars at the playground and
Can you imagine a husband and wife

On the titter totter or a man of
Business on the merry-go-round so no
It's OK to watch the kids or grandkids
Who don't have a thought about how they look

Who think its funny to get dizzy or
Silly but adults must be dignified.

So what's up with the
water-skiers and surfers
bungee-cord jumpers
the hikers and skydivers —
what's with the rollercoaster?

I want to be left alone thank you I
Sometimes think to myself especially
When focusing on the radio or
A task as I have expectations of

People for the things I want them to do
For me and ordinarily there's the
Give and take of cooking and cleaning and
Mowing the grass and paying bills that are

Obvious but there's also a subtle
Measuring of emotional service
Whether I'm receiving what's due me and
It is probable I don't even know

The demands I'm making on those I love
Because I don't see my expectations.

And it's funny how
needy I can be without
knowing it and it's
so funny what everyone
expects without saying so.

My mind today is predominately
A grayish sky the rain is falling from
But I'm not unhappy I'm savoring
A chilly day in a warming season

A burst of rain followed by quietness
The leaves growing to fullness and not yet
Nibbled by the insects and I do take
Pleasure in each of three shades of lilac

Blossoms in the hedge that I planted so
Many years ago and don't remember
Noticing before now and noticing
Is the trick I've learned during a season

Of living that rain or shine whatever
I'm right on the edge of transformation.

I'm not separate
from anything I see I'm
predominately
a vessel of sensations
navigating mystery.

Roses in poetry have become trite
As everyone has written of the folds
Within folds within folds and contrasted
Petals with thorns as if the beauty and

The sharpness had a point but during most
Of the year the rose bush consists of stems
And little leaves and yes the bloom in spring
Is lovely emerging in a shower

Of sunlight within a season bursting
With growth and for some reason poets do
Keep writing about roses — more so than
Chrysanthemums — as if a rose were a

Sight to behold like the sun and the moon
And in beholding a rose I am caught.

So there is something
about the bloom of a rose
like the sun and moon
captivating enchanting
eyes capable of seeing.

I'm lucky I've heard anger is a form
Of suffering as it's necessary
To stand apart and watch it's effects to
See destructive qualities — I'm lucky

To be with a group that values kindness
Because cherishing hatreds together
Against opposing groups could override
My capacity for careful thinking —

As anger fixes on a target and
Burns the heart and the intellect will find
Justifications and who hasn't known
Justifiable anger and villains

But not enough people recognize how
Blinding obsessive anger can become.

I know it's my job
to experience anger
to suffer anger
enough to desire a
more careful way to live.

A stone a rose and an apple appear and
The stone fits within my palm weighty and
Smooth with curving contours and a flatter
Side minutely pitted and the petals

Of the yellow rose are silky between
My fingers and the tip of a thorn is
Sharp on my thumb and I gaze at the folds
In folds in folds of the blossom and the

Apple is red and yellow and the skin
Is crisp and the fruit is tasty and I
Take a bite as big as I can manage
And discover I'm quite hungry and just

These simple pastimes are enough for now —
I don't have to let my mind cogitate.

Sometimes I love to
touch the surface of a stone
see the rose's bloom
eat an entire apple
return to simplicity.

Monkey Mind

His guru had one more suggestion as
He was leaving saying "one thing you must not
Do when meditating this week think about
Monkeys" and how easy thought the student

As these creatures never crossed his mind but
This week while sitting his thoughts exploded
With somber gorillas toothy baboons
Monkeys with red bottoms and rambunctious

Scampering chattering even shrieking
Chimpanzees and he was angry with his
Master saying "You did this purposely
Your instructions not to think about them

Made it likely I would think about them"
And smiling the guru said "now you see."

And so with any
difficulty trying to
escape certain thoughts
doesn't make them go away
but only makes them stronger.

Matt's a six-foot banana today on
The sidewalk and might have been Gumby a
Coke bottle or Spiderman yesterday
And he's standing and driving a Segway

A T-shaped vehicle with two wheels and
He was a soldier in Afghanistan
Was shot in the head has memory loss
And headaches and because he can't work he

Passes the time in a costume looking
Ridiculous to snare the attention
Of passersby attempting to impart
Happiness because he intends to turn

Around a bad day someone is having
Because his humor is the best of him.

It's too easy
to become isolated
laughter is magic
humor communicates and
people need inspiration.

I liked the upright posture of the seat
Because I stayed alert while driving and
It's smallness made turning zippy and the
Compact windshield was right-sized and over

The years it became such a familiar
Pleasure as natural as putting on
A jacket and going anywhere as
Easily as walking and the trips my

Family took the daily motion of
My life adhered to the PT Cruiser
So when the electronics failed the cost
Of its repair soared reluctantly I

Decided to trade it for whatever
I could — I turned my back and walked away.

Things I've acquired
are material objects
tools of convenience
but my enthusiasm
encompasses everything.

Hot Wheels

As a child I loved toys especially
Collectables and I gathered dozens
Of small cars with pin axels allowing
Their wheels to spin easily and each was

Precious and when I see a specific
Shade of yellow I yearn for one of my
Lost possessions but at the Toyota
Dealership I could only choose one so

I chose a Corolla because I love
It's size style and reputed quality
And I wavered between a choice of black
Or red and was partly determined by

The newer tires on the one I bought but
I was captivated by its candy red.

Do I possess the
car or does it possess me?
Could I do without
possessions or am I a
captive of collectables?

I see how Bill Elliot's converted
The gas station on the corner into a
Two-story home with a stairway to
The roof and a railing on the top for

Gazing about when the warmth returns and
Sometimes he meanders around without
A shirt exhibiting his extra pounds
His ponytail with nonchalance and with

Apparent leisure and I do admire
His decoration of the waist-high wrought
Iron fence with blue green silver and red
Pinwheels because he's perceptive because

The spinning wheels in spring are becoming
Because they do complement the blossoms.

Disregarding the
conventional taking
different paths and
using imagination
is the American dream.

In Stillwater

While I'm sitting on a wall designed to
Hold a river rising with the flood of
Springtime I'm seeing the distance to the
Limestone bluffs on the other side of the

Valley watching as the undulating
Water on the surface sparkles in waves
Disconnected from the direction of
What must be a massive current moving

To an ocean and I'm allowing my
Mind to settle with the tiny waves as
If the movement and my thoughts were one thing
For the time being with the sun on my

Face and then I realize how much like
The water I am always in motion.

As my thoughts are
settling and my blood is
circulating and
my heart is beating I'm not
even lifting a finger.

The accelerator and the steering
Are automatic — the four lanes and the
Sparse traffic are perfect for swift passage
Over the rolling hills of Wisconsin

Under a sky dotted all the way to
The horizon with clouds — and farms and trees
Arise flowing indistinguishably
In a vast and constant procession and

I'm consuming distance by watching the
Mammoth trucks I pass and by seeing a
Singularly tall hill that's twenty miles
Ahead that is surprisingly modest

As it vanishes off to my right and
Becomes predictably forgettable.

In a tangle of
construction in Green Bay
I missed a turn and
consternation swearing and
sweat predominated.

The Trick

Don't be hypnotized by these words because
This poem is a manipulation
And the letters and the syllables were
Measured for the creation of cadence

Selected for the accentuation
Of sounds pleasing both the ears and eyes as
You may read or hear these lines and each word
Carries only an approximation

Of meaning and the words aren't true but
They point to a reality beyond words —
I take the time in the morning to touch
The sunrise with my eyes and the rising

Sun dissolves the tensions of yesterday
And I'm titillated with its beauty.

The waves of sunlight
bedazzle my senses and
just for a moment
this ordinary morning
is extraordinary.

The retaining wall was bulging and would
Not have stood another season so we
Disassembled blocks put aside busted
Pieces and shoveled a new foundation

And we carved into the bank — making a
Pile of dirt — and we spread pea gravel to
Establish a level base and stretched a
Taut line for guidance and as the sun blazed

We placed new blocks of a sturdier type
Below and replaced the undamaged blocks
Layer on layer and for fill behind
The wall we dumped pea gravel and broken

Stone with the intention that water would
Pass between the fill and blocks harmlessly.

The neighbor wanted
the extra dirt and we used
her mini-tractor
and a trailer shoveling
it in and spreading it out.

Poetics

Aristotle supposed that music has
A civilizing or a barbarous
Influence and who would argue the point
That listening to a symphony in

A hall designed for resonance doesn't
Impart refinement but such wasn't the
Setting I encountered last night with the
Pulsating syrupy blues playing good

And loud and there I sat struggling with
The urge and embarrassment of looking
Foolish that I overcame to become
Again the whirling dervish of thirty

Years ago as the music took me from
 Self-consciousness to such joy in motion.

Taken completely
with raw pulsating rhythm
without melody
I simply became music
without a care in my head.

There's nothing selfish about it and it's
Necessary to practice ignoring
My nagging conscience saying I should be
Sad because you're sad or share your anger

With someone else and when I've done something
To precipitate your anger I catch
Myself becoming angry denying
Blame and feeling guilty too because I

Have no surety for judging so I
Breathe calming breaths and become a little
Distant from you perhaps leaving the room
Because I want to be the captain of

My emotions in a ship with enough
Ballast to weather the difficult seas.

It's not possible
to be compassionate if
I'm just reacting
so I really do need to
discover my surety.

Just for today I am the breeze in the
Trees I am the sound of peace and I am
Breath visible in the leaves and I am
A sparrow on a twig for a moment

And just for today I am the warm sun
On the skin of my legs and I am the
Clarity of light in the valley and
I am the glimmer and sparkle of the

Sun on the river and just for today
I am undulating water I am
The sounds of the cars rising in the
Air in the city I am the faces

And the voices of the people passing
By on the street just for today I am.

I am forgetful
I am forgiveness today
I am the morning
I am the moment without
anticipation or fear.

Impetuosity is a spaniel
Bounding and turning in the grass without
Hesitation as he's free to roam and
Romp and lunge and dart and taste and smell to

Satisfaction until he's exhausted
With exuberance and what a joy it
Is to watch such rollicking expression
With a tinge perhaps of envy as I

Recognize if I behaved that way they'd
Lock me up and anyway I've acquired
Prohibitions and inhibitions and
My appearance needs consideration

And I have consequences to beware —
I've lost the innocence of ignorance.

My inner spaniel
talks and laughs and reads and writes
and exercises
I'm free to roam and to romp
and to write any damn thing.

As the years are accumulating the
Seasons are becoming precious to me
And in the transition from winter I
Watched the tips of trees begin to bud

And noticed the vulnerability
And the beseeching posture of the limbs
Rising up to the sun but now in the
Summer their forms are concealed within

Luxuriant foliage and I'm attuned
To the ascending and dissipating
Sound of the wind in the leaves just as if
The trees are sighing and I remember

These voices from childhood resonating
Communicating succoring soothing.

The invisible
undulating in the trees
the inaudible
arising within the leaves
communicating soothing.

Proximity

As if my thoughts were secrets only I
Should know as if my secrets were precious
Separating you from me defining
Our differences establishing borders

But it doesn't matter that I'm quiet
And you're boisterous I'm doubtful and you're
Confident that people come to you and
I'm often alone because I am not

Alone and though I choose to be quiet
And separate my thoughts and emotions
Are communal and secrets meaningless —
A person lives with the nourishment of

Love and dies in isolation and so
I have to practice communication.

No one lives alone
separateness is deadly
and to be happy
I have to discover how
to communicate with you.

A weighty can of peaches fell from the
Shelf and broke her toe and she was angry
With me because I put it up where it
Could fall and yes I knew the door of the

Closet's sticky and needs a determined
Jerk but I couldn't have known her hefty
Yank would agitate the peaches and break
Her toe but it did and I'm familiar

With the fun of reactionary rage
And I could've become angry too but
For some reason that day I didn't and
Discovered I don't have to play the game

It's not necessary to react with
Anger and I'm quite capable of poise.

While I'm not happy
the peaches broke her toe I'll
remember the day
when I could've been angry
but instead learned to be kind.

After an hour of sleep I woke to hear
The minutest whine of a mosquito
Just about my ear so I took a swipe
But missed and slapped my ear instead and then

I lay awake listening and hearing it
Coming near and going away and I
Almost fell asleep again but there it
Was and I slapped my ear again and missed

So I turned on the lights and looked about
Determined for blood but as it was the
Smallest mosquito it couldn't be seen
So I lay in bed listening breathing

On the verge of sleep and jolting awake
Because of this tiniest irritant.

This morning is the
clearest and deepest kind of
blue sky but I am
woozy and wondering why
we must have mosquitoes.
.

I'm not over it yet and there's no use
Pretending I am as I think about
The way you seduced me by being coy
And vulnerable and asking for my

Help appealing to my libido as
Much as my vanity and ignorance
As you are perceptive and skilled and yet
I'm grateful for the discoveries you

Generated that love and passion are
Different — passion is a great force and
Love is a need for the deepest sharing
And passion is addictive while love is

A calling a metamorphosis and
I discovered how to love selflessly.

I gave away
my secrets and desires
you knew my thoughts and
though you weren't trustworthy
I learned to share everything.

The torque of its motor is impressive
In the morning darkness as I'm in bed
As the rumbling behemoth arrives
And stops and as a mechanical whine

Begins as I know its arm is clamping
The container and lifting as I hear
Clinking clunking rattling evidence
Of trash settling on trash and then I

Hear the whine and then the rumbling as
The leviathan departs with its so
Odiferous cargo supplemented
With my modest offerings and I think

How wonderful it is at my leisure
To be observing civilization.

We each have a role
and we acquire the most
exquisite talents
with such specialized tools all
for the benefit of all.

I had to remind myself as I was
Lying on my side with my elbow bent
Above my head for a very long hour
That this was a voluntary ordeal

And the application of the thickest
Needles for outlining was the most
Excruciating and I doubted I could
Stand it but once the job's begun there's no

Turning back so I reminded myself
I adored the peacock feather as a
Symbol worthy of intimacy so
I shut my eyes and endured the needles —

Tattooing on the ribs is tortuous
But not torture if you're asking for it.

Usually it's
over when it's over but
I had determined
to return the following
day to do the other side.

Youth and ignorance aren't an advantage
For selecting the first tattoo because
Without experience there's no context
For judging and in my case I became

Excited and decided without much
Thinking and so in Galveston Texas
Harpoon Barry incised an odious
Swallow on my chest I wore shamefully

But a tattoo should inspire with a
Resonant meaning and beforehand it
Should be visualized precisely where
It's to be and the artist shouldn't be

Any stray dog but should be respected
With a portfolio of work to show.

The embarrassing
swallow was majestically
overlaid with an
eagle in a flurry and
a festival of motion.

Even on a cloudy day in summer
There is radiance penetrating as
I go about my life inattentive of
Its presence sustaining me even as

The rain is falling in sheets and water
Is flowing on the streets on the way to
The river there is radiance moving
Ceaselessly nourishing me even in

The middle of the night as I'm dreaming
Under a panorama of stars and
A half moon there is unsurpassable
Radiance coursing in my veins and in

The morning the sun rises again to
Compose the day with brilliant energy

The enveloping
animating radiance
of the weighty sun
is ceaselessly burning and
showering the earth with life.

Because water flows from high to low and
Because the water happened to flow in
Arizona in one direction the
Canyons were carved for thousands of years and

To me they appear beautiful but when
The pressure accumulates along the
Fault lines of the Earth's crust and suddenly
There's a break underwater and a surge

Of the ocean overwhelms a coastal
Village in Japan and people and homes
Are caught in a wall of water and swept
Out to sea as the water returns

To me it's horrible to be against
Unpredictable all consuming force.

There's not a hint of
of the precariousness
of life or of the
massive power of water
in a single drifting cloud.
.

With a red nose and watery eyes with
A hazy dizziness in the way of
Easy thought I endured forty summers
Of allergic frustration and though I

Didn't die and compensated with a
Plethora of handkerchiefs I would have
Eagerly traded noses but then a
Clever specialist spotted the polyps

In my nasal cavities and he zapped them
With steroids and now my daily sprays
Are working and I may go anywhere
With a dry nose and a clear head and with

Eyes liberated but sometimes I
Regret the time saturated with sneezes.

I could've been an
intellectual or a
foolish romantic
could've traveled anywhere —
I could've been a hero.

The apex of the summer is passing
The power of the sun is lessening
The light is becoming golden gilding
The leaves and the grass — and the air is a

Medley of cool and warm — and in the late
Afternoon though the sun may swelter with
Fierceness it doesn't last long and as the
Sun is setting earlier a chill is

Emerging at night and it's easier
To sleep under covers with the windows
Open with a chorus of crickets in
The breezes and I'm not tossing in bed

In the muggy air because late summer
Is the absolute pinnacle for dreams.

Blue skies arise in
every season but the earth
responds differently
as the sun cooperates
with the earth's revolutions.

The St. Croix Crossing Bridge

For fifty years we've been arguing and
Having lawsuits about spanning the St.
Croix River Valley with a new bridge
And it took a congressional vote and

A president's signature to sweep
Aside opposition and vast swaths of
Earth have been moved and deep piers established
Through the mucky bottom into bedrock

So in the air over a distance a
Steel and concrete form aerodynamic
And graceful has risen representing
A modern monument of beautiful

Lines with utilitarian purpose
And traffic will hum over the valley.

We don't have the time
to dawdle on scenery
we're driven by the
necessity to keep up
with the pace of our email.

Trilling far off and throbbing nearby the
Crickets are blanketing the darkness with
Sound and if I were slumbering wouldn't
They be whispering messages of peace

And wouldn't I have forgotten worries
And wouldn't I be with my companions
And perhaps the rhythm of the crickets
Would become music and celebration

But I can't escape nervousness and my
Thoughts are churning uselessly and my
Eyes are burning holes in the night but as
Weary as I am I return again

And again to the evidence of the
Crickets — there's really no need to worry.

On the edge of sleep
I don't care where I am or
struggle with problems
because I'm traveling and
don't even know who I am.

In the middle of August while driving
In Stillwater I notice the tips of
The leaves are coloring as I'm wearing
A t-shirt and don't remember when the

Seasons usually turn and because
It's muggy this afternoon it's hard to
Imagine snow — but on the driveway I
See a red maple leaf and realize

Summer doesn't last — so I look for the
Tree and become familiar again with
The neighborhood and find the maple and
See a sprinkling of red at the top

And remember this tree every autumn
Becomes the epitome of crimson.

I remember the
the maple trees in Kyoto
grow miniature leaves
that present the perfection
of autumn crimson brilliance.

When we moved in twenty years ago there
Were fleas to exterminate and water
Was seeping into the basement but there
Was a furnace a washer a dryer

And a refrigerator and over
Years we tore out carpet re-shingled the
Roof replaced the water heater and the
Roots of the cottonwood tree busted the

Sewage pipe costing thousands of dollars
To repair while I've been watching as the
Kids got taller and outgrew taking the
Bus to school and came home on holidays

From college and while they've moved away the
Structure of home contains the memories.

It's easy to
dry-vac basement
water but as
the driveway wears
puddles get bigger.

Avalokiteshvara

The one comprehending the suffering
Of everyone having a thousand eyes
And hands who is compassionate who is
Moved to alleviate the suffering

Of so much and so many such a one
Would be invisibly and ceaselessly
Acting everywhere within and without —
While I understand so little of the

Suffering I inflame of myself and
Others while in agitation I ask
Why in the world the bodhisattva is
Necessary while I resist coming

To embody compassion myself how
Is liberation even possible?

I believe in
simplicity
sincerity
and want to be
compassionate.

As if it were an emissary from
Paradise the peacock arises in
This world where people suffer accidents
Disease violence where the spirit is

Vulnerable to pain exhaustion and
Depression it comes with opalescent
Green and blue and bronze it promenades with
A fan of voluptuous feathers each

With a regal core of purple and how
Do we reconcile inescapable
Difficulty with inexplicable
Beauty except to believe there is more

To living than we can appreciate
And the peacock is a hint of marvels.

Like children see
the beauty of the peacock
the bloom of the rose
the majesty of mountains
the splendor of sunrises.

It is possible to take pleasure in
The everyday experience of the
Sun — but while driving I was listening
To commentary on the radio

About a celebrity who was at
A restaurant having lunch and because
The politics of the famous diner
Were prominent and controversial

A server doused the diner with a glass
Of water and the personalities
On the radio were offended by
The praise the server was enjoying on

Snapchat on Twitter and on Facebook —
Gleeful virtuous congratulations.

My mind is a bowl
open to cottonwood leaves
dancing in a breeze
but now I am distracted
and sunlight is out of reach.

The silhouette of me on the sidewalk
Walking ahead synchronized perfectly
With every motion of my body is
Spooky as I'm seeing my shadow self

As a symbol not of who I am now
But of whom I previously could have
Been in other lifetimes or of whom I
Could become if I let myself go far

Enough because I'm a dynamo of
Elasticity and when driven by
Drug addiction I trespassed boundaries
I never expected to cross and in

Recovery I discovered I am
Capable of genuine compassion.

I am a walking
potentiality for
better or worse or
an indifferent mixture
depending on my choices.

We go to the sanctuary of the
Church early in the morning just as the
Sun is lighting the stained glass windows and
We practice walking meditation by

Ceaselessly carefully taking small steps
Following each other in silence and
Synchronizing our steps and breaths as well
As possible mixing Zen within a

Setting of Christian artistry with the
Intention of sharing the moment with
Settled minds and simple motion and the
Quiet presence in the sanctuary

Reminds me I don't have to hurry and
It's quite possible to embody peace.

The green blue red gold
Purple and yellow of the
Stained glass windows are
Variously dim or bright
Depending on the season.

As we do our walking meditation
In the sanctuary of the church we
Try to synchronize our steps and breaths with
Each other to achieve harmony and

Simplicity and openness and I
See a stained glass window with an ark and
A dove curving vines and leaves illumined
By the rising sun and there's a plaque of

Dedication to Tom Phillips — who was
Pastor of the church — to his wife Percy —
And I recall his persistent kindness
And his quiet watchfulness in this place

And I realize stepping carefully
Is exerting comforting influence.

The memorials
are visible reminders
designed for seeing
and perpetuating love
but memory perishes.

I'm ambivalent about having a
Memory as it's loaded with regrets
And wounds and also victories that I've
Transformed to triumphs I use to measure

Myself against others and the past is
Filtered through my story-telling machine
Because I want to ascribe meaning to
Events because I do need a sense of

Direction but how I determine to
Remember a friendship that dissolved and
Hurt is paramount because it's easy
To be a victim nourishing anger

Preventing spontaneous forgiveness
And making compassion impossible.

I do remember
as I choose to remember
and my choices are
determinate so I need
to practice circumspection.

The Mirror

It's just glass with a solid backing yet
It's acquired magical quality
Reflecting perfectly anyone who
Comes before it so what is its value

In an empty room with no one looking
As it's like a box without a lid as
It's not complete without a consciousness
Apprehending its visions and we who

Come before it should beware because it
Casts a spell by implying the image
Is the self when really it's the ego
Seeing the ego evaluating

Cherishing or disparaging so we
Go away deluded about ourselves.

Imagine living
without knowing how you look
how differently would
you think about yourself and
is it even possible?

The Person in the Mirror

Imagine yourself on a journey of
Consecutive lifetimes and with every
Birth comes different parents and siblings
And economic circumstances and

Alternating genders and a new face
And differences in strength and health and in
Grace of body and acuity of
Mind and in each instance you adapt

As well as you may with gathered or with
Dissipated confidence perceiving
Either oppression or well being and
Desiring accomplishment and praise

So when you gaze at you in the mirror
Do you recognize basic consciousness?

Suppose death is a
turning of circumstances
a rearrangement
of superficial facts — how
much of you comes with you?

Imagine having coffee with one of
Your friends and the deity played a joke
And transformed both of you so you would be
Looking at your face with your friend's eyes and

Your memory and habits were within
Her body and though the voice expressing
Your surprise would be quite familiar it's
Not what you're used to as it's a woman's

And you were a man — could you go home to
Her family or would you return to your
Wife with her body because how could you
Walk into someone else's life and know

How to behave because more than just a
Body the universe would be scrambled?

Can the body and
consciousness be divided?
Can the universe
that creates incarnation
really be comprehended?

The Way

Do I have the power to be happy
In my ways of relating with people
In my habits within the convergence
Of circumstances when I find myself

Opposed to someone or suffering from
Illness or difficulty how do I
Cope when my choices are complex and fraught
With uncertainty when what I want seems

Unobtainable and what I possess
Unbearable am I able to sleep
In the pivotal periods before
Resolution and do I realize

My eyes aren't unique and everyone more
Or less encounters the dark and the light?

Am I possessed by
my emotions or have I
found the practices
for equanimity and
compassionate engagement?

How could a life be evaluated
Without considering relationships
In marriages and friendships and working
Partnerships because we are designed for

Communication and our different
Talents and often antagonistic
Perspectives do produce society —
It's a mystery to me why the friend

I knew to be available and kind
For twelve years became cold and evasive
Without explanation and I grieve the
Absence of a friend — and I resent the

Presence of the stranger my friend became
Because now I'm missing conversation.

I do create
stories about
failed friendships
and I want to
be big hearted.

The autumn colors are extinguished and
Bare trees are waving in a steady wind
And I remember here in this room my
Dad stumbled backwards hitting his head

On the tile and I lifted from behind
With my arms under his getting him up
Dazed — I don't remember how we got him
To the hospital and it was only

A single event in a series of
Accidents and illnesses marking an
Irreversible decline but very
Often when visiting I saw him propped

Up in different hospital beds cheerful
As if he were taking a vacation.

I remember Dad
in the hospital
hospitable
welcoming
visitors.

The streets are stark again as I'm driving
And seeing the overcast sky through bare
Branches again that arrived yesterday
And there's the carcass of a squirrel on

The road being jabbed by several crows and
And I can't help missing the other birds
And I remember the summer foliage
And I pass the crabapple trees that bloom

In spring — but Thanksgiving is coming soon
And then Christmas and New Year's Day and I
Will take the opportunity to wear
My colorful fleece shirts that I only

Wear in winter and I'm doing my best
To savor diminished sunlight again.

It's a season
of celebrations
of companionship
of expressions of
enthusiasm.

A good home is filled with memories of
Thanksgivings Christmases and Easters when
Everyone gathered to discuss the news
And the feasts were prepared with the skills of

Accumulated years and I never
Really leave but carry the loving through
Life as a foundation to build on but
When I enter in again the chair where

My dad sat the couch where he napped and the
Painting that watched over him are tinged with
Sadness as recollections of his hives
His faintings and his slow decline are now

Inseparable with the fact nothing
Lasts forever not even memory.

In a home every
item carries memories
of its origin
of how it came to its place
and of who would care for it.

This winter I'm seeing the naked trees
And remembering I will be sixty
Years old in November but I'm lucky
Because I don't feel my age and because

Of my exercise I'm as spry as a
Teenager — but I have wrinkles about
My eyes and I have memories also
And as I'm driving and seeing the bare

Branches of the trees overhanging the
Street I remember the cathedrals in
England I saw when I was a student
And realize that the stone tracery

In those churches are meant to represent
The graceful lines of trees in the winter.

I'm sometimes
surprised by
eyesight
memory
and insight.

Asthma

I'm sitting still but chugging right along
Like a company of Greek warriors
Plying their oars in battle because two
Days ago I acquired a cough that

Would not let go and though I go to the
Gym everyday doing cardio work
At night in bed my coughing continued
With equal determination so I

Visited a doctor and he prescribed
Prednisone to fight the inflammation
In my lungs and so the circulation
Of my blood is throbbing as if I were

At the gym on a machine but I'm not
Lifting a finger while smiting the cough.

I imagine the
predicament of having
a persistent cough
while not having a doctor
and not having Prednisone.

I'm grateful for the asphalt because if
My driveway were gravel I'd be blowing
It away bit by bit and I'm happy
To have my sturdy snow blower because

No matter how prodigious the dump it
Plods along spewing the snow to the side
And I can swivel the direction of
The spray by turning a handle because

I don't want to blow into a fierce wind
Because my face would get crusted with the
Snow and as long as the temperature
Stays well below freezing I'll be OK

Because if the snow warms to slushiness
The snow blower clogs and then I shovel.

It's not much fun
thrusting away with
a loaded shovel
with snow sticking
to the metal.

— *Tekkan*

www.ingramcontent.com/pod-product-compliance
Lightning Source LLC
Chambersburg PA
CBHW052103070526
44584CB00017B/2310